...anic
...liners

Tony Romo

Star Quarterback

Zella Williams

PowerKiDS
press

New York

Published in 2011 by The Rosen Publishing Group, Inc.
29 East 21st Street, New York, NY 10010

First Edition

Editor: Joanne Randolph
Book Design: Kate Laczynski
Photo Researcher: Jessica Gerweck

Photo Credits: Cover, p. 1 Scott Boehm/Getty Images; p. 4 Elsa/Getty Images; p. 5 Chris McGrath/ Getty Images; pp. 6–7, 20 Al Messerschmidt/Getty Images; pp. 8–9 © Brad Horn/AP Images; p. 10, 11 © Morry Gash/AP Images; p. 12 © Alan Look/Icon SMI; p. 13 Collegiate Images/Getty Images; pp. 14–15, 16 © Donna McWilliam/AP Images; p. 17 Stephen Dunn/Getty Images; pp. 18, 19 (top) © Tony Gutierrez/AP Images; p. 19 (bottom) Drew Hallowell/Getty Images; p. 21 Paul Spinelli/Getty Images; p. 22 Michael P. Malarkey/Getty Images.

Library of Congress Cataloging-in-Publication Data

Williams, Zella.
  Tony Romo : star quarterback / Zella Williams. — 1st ed.
     p. cm.
  Includes index.
  ISBN 978-1-4488-1456-5 (library binding) — ISBN 978-1-4488-1476-3 (pbk.) — ISBN 978-1-4488-1477-0 (6-pack)
  1. Romo, Tony, 1980—Juvenile literature. 2. Football players—United States–Biography— Juvenile literature. 3. Quarterbacks (Football—United States—Biography—Juvenile literature. I. Title.
  GV939.R646W55 2011
  796.332092—dc22
  [B]
                                      2010001389

Manufactured in the United States of America

CPSIA Compliance Information: Batch #WS10PK: For Further Information contact Rosen Publishing, New York, New York at 1-800-237-9932

CONTENTS

Antonio Ramiro "Tony" Romo is a quarterback in the National Football League (NFL). This Hispanic **athlete** did not get to play much in the first part of his

Since 2006, Romo has been 1 of the top 10 starting quarterbacks in the NFL.

Here Romo makes a pass to a teammate. He has broken many records as a Cowboys quarterback.

professional football career. He worked hard during those early years and soon earned a starting spot. Since then, he has become a star quarterback!

Tony Romo was born on April 21, 1980, in San Diego, California. His father, Ramiro Romo, served in the U.S. Navy. His mother, Joan, worked in a supermarket to make extra money.

Tony Romo is a Mexican American. Ramiro Romo Sr., his grandfather, moved to Texas from Mexico as a teenager.

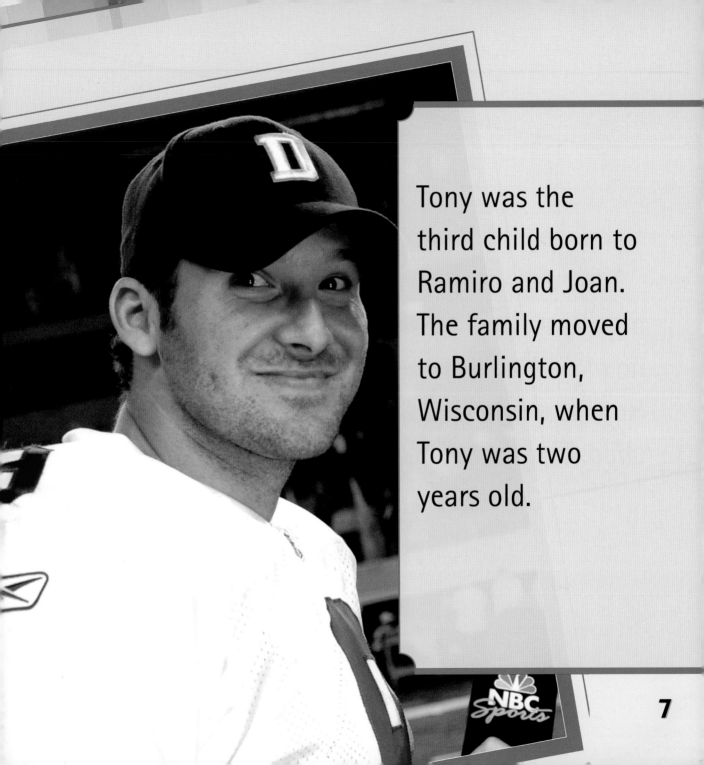

Tony was the
third child born to
Ramiro and Joan.
The family moved
to Burlington,
Wisconsin, when
Tony was two
years old.

Tony enjoyed sports from a young age. Basketball was his first love, but he played many other sports as well. He was a **talented** athlete even as a child. Tony began playing Little League

Tony Romo gets paid to play football, but he loves to play golf in his free time.

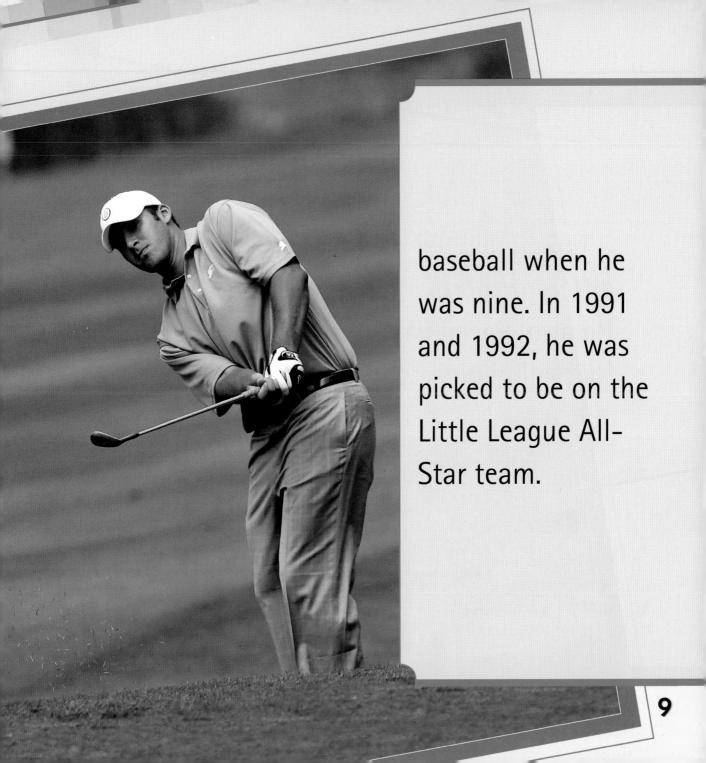

baseball when he was nine. In 1991 and 1992, he was picked to be on the Little League All-Star team.

Tony Romo did well playing many different sports. He enjoyed golf and tennis. He also played **varsity** basketball and football in high school. Romo was starting

Today Burlington High School students can see Tony Romo's jersey as they walk to class.

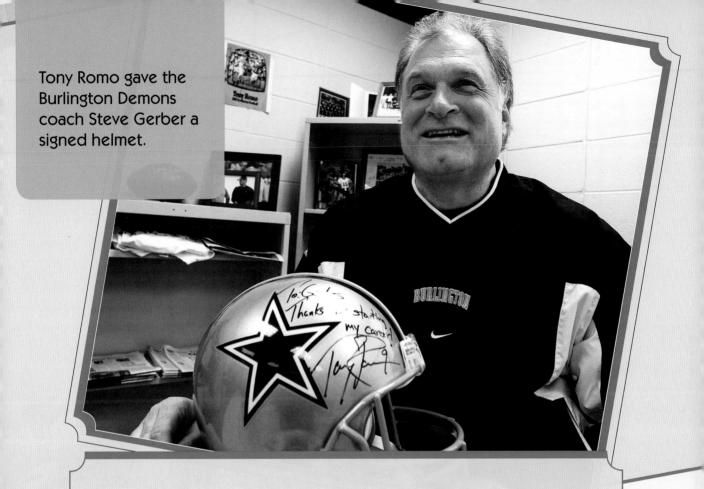

Tony Romo gave the Burlington Demons coach Steve Gerber a signed helmet.

quarterback for the Burlington Demons in his junior and senior years. He had planned to play soccer, but there were not enough players for a team!

In 1999, Tony Romo went to Eastern Illinois University, in Charleston, Illinois. He played for the Panthers football team there. He became the all-time touchdown leader

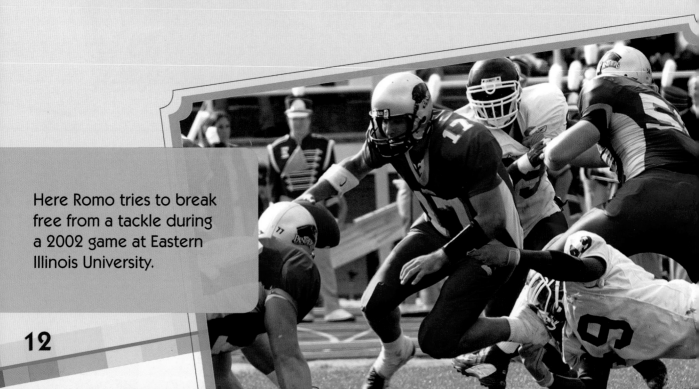

Here Romo tries to break free from a tackle during a 2002 game at Eastern Illinois University.

In 2009, Eastern Illinois retired Romo's jersey. This means that no one else can wear the number 17 there.

in his **division**. He also won the Walter Payton Award. This award is given to the best player in Division 1AA football.

Many college football players hope to get **drafted** by a professional football team. Romo was no different. On draft day in 2003, he spoke with five NFL teams, including the Dallas Cowboys,

Here Bill Parcells talks to Romo during training camp in 2003, after he entered the NFL.

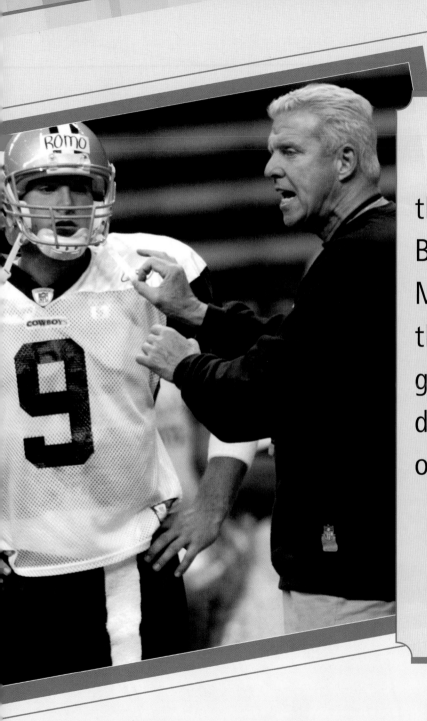

the Denver
Broncos, and the
Miami Dolphins. In
the end, he did not
get drafted. Romo's
dream was not
over, though.

Tony Romo was soon offered a chance to play for the Dallas Cowboys. He worked hard for this team. He started off as a third-string quarterback. This meant he did

Tony Romo came to training camp in 2003 as one of three quarterbacks for the Cowboys.

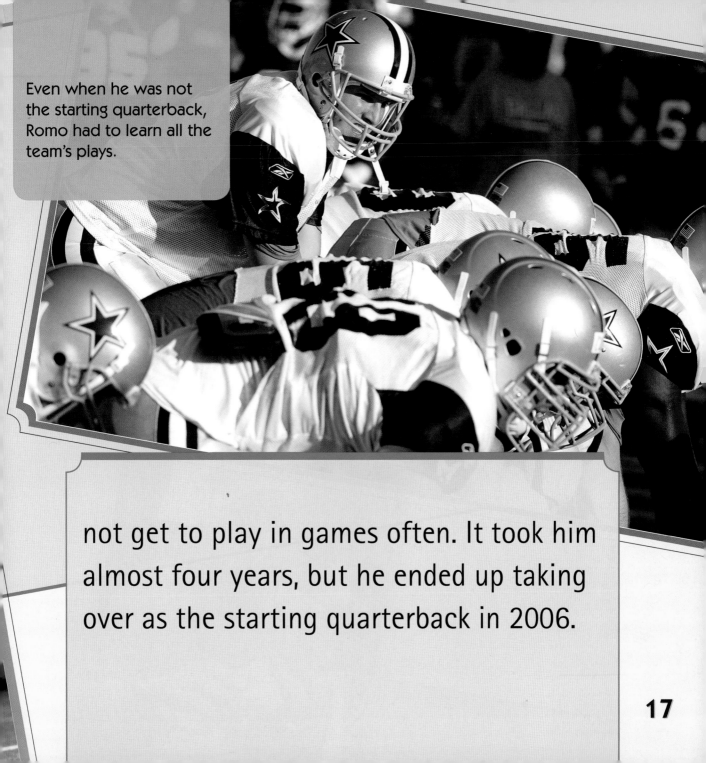

Even when he was not the starting quarterback, Romo had to learn all the team's plays.

not get to play in games often. It took him almost four years, but he ended up taking over as the starting quarterback in 2006.

Romo made the most of his chance to shine. As starting quarterback in 2006, Romo led the Cowboys to the play-offs. He played well in 2007 and

In an October 2008 game, Romo broke his little finger. He could not play for about a month.

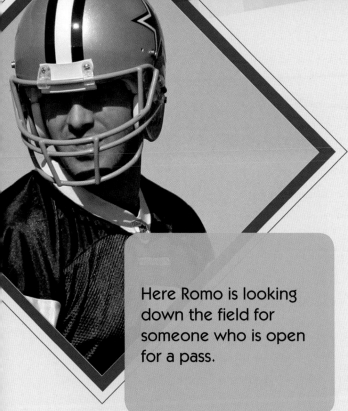

Here Romo is looking down the field for someone who is open for a pass.

led the team to 13 wins that season. This tied the Cowboys' record for most wins in a season. In 2009, the team made it to the play-offs, too.

Romo needs to tell the other players on the field what the plan is.

Tony Romo has set many records. He also has won many awards. In college, he was the best player in his division. He held the record for most touchdown passes in

Tony Romo led his team to a spot in the play-offs in January 2010.

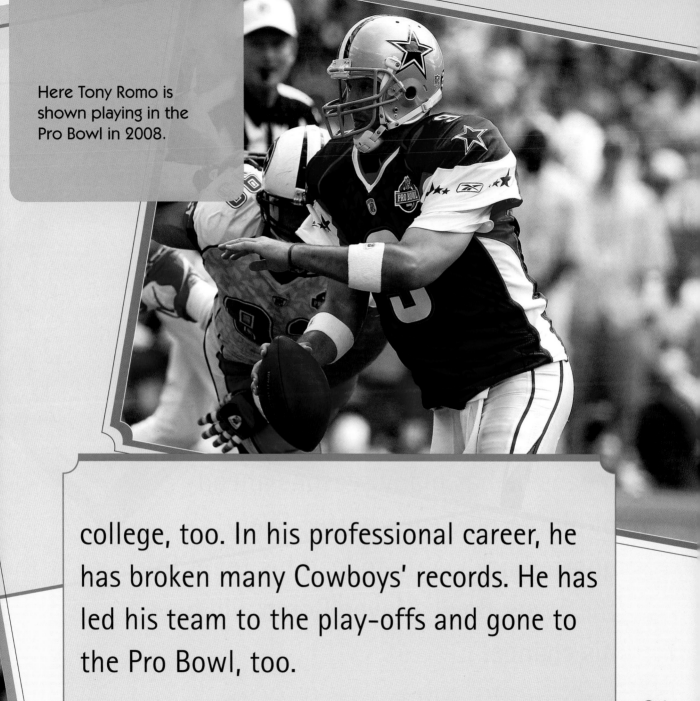

Here Tony Romo is shown playing in the Pro Bowl in 2008.

college, too. In his professional career, he has broken many Cowboys' records. He has led his team to the play-offs and gone to the Pro Bowl, too.

What is ahead for Tony Romo? You will have to watch him to find out! He signed a **contract** to play for the Cowboys at least through 2013. That

means he has many seasons ahead of him to play even better. Every quarterback wants to lead his team to the Super Bowl. Maybe Romo will have his chance!

GLOSSARY

athlete (ATH-leet) Someone who takes part in sports.

contract (KAHN-trakt) An agreement between two or more people.

division (dih-VIH-zhun) A group or department.

drafted (DRAFT-ed) Picked for a special purpose or job.

talented (TA-lent-ed) Skilled.

varsity (VAR-sih-tee) The main team in a high school sport.

INDEX

A
athlete, 4, 8

B
basketball, 8, 10
Burlington,
    Wisconsin, 7

C
career, 5, 21
child, 7–8
contract, 22

D
division, 13, 20

F
family, 7

G
golf, 10

N
National Football
    League (NFL), 4

R
Romo, Joan
    (mother), 6–7
Romo, Ramiro
    (father), 6–7

S
San Diego,
    California, 6
sports, 8, 10

T
team(s), 9, 11–12,
    14, 16, 19, 21–22
tennis, 10

U
U.S. Navy, 6

V
varsity, 10

WEB SITES

Due to the changing nature of Internet links, PowerKids Press has developed an online list of Web sites related to the subject of this book. This site is updated regularly. Please use this link to access the list: www.powerkidslinks.com/hh/romo/